DEAR M♥THER

DEAR MTHER

POEMS ON THE HOT MESS OF MOTHERHOOD

BUNMI LADITAN

mira

mira

ISBN-13: 978-0-7783-0846-1

Dear Mother

to the One who loves me
and knows me by name

CONTENTS

LOVE

Where can you find my heart?
It is no longer locked away
afraid of the cold world.
You won't find it racing to
keep up with what strangers want me to be.
Nor is it attached to my sleeve
ready to be broken by
a harsh word or glance.
My heart can be found
hidden
in the small, plump hand
of this child I call mine
who cares not what I look like
or have achieved
but wants only
to rest in my arms
until dawn breaks.

DEAR MOTHER

The audacity of a child's

demands for love

are only matched

by the ridiculous depths

of the love their parents

have for them

What kind of magic enchants
the well of motherhood?
Mere hours after my ragged
bucket scraped the last
drops of mercy from the
echoey depths
I find myself
once again
at my child's bedside
hypnotized by a face
so breathtakingly serene
And as I slide my hand
across the softest of cheeks
somewhere inside me
I feel the waters
that hours ago had been depleted
begin to rise

DEAR MOTHER

Most days I wake up tired
No longer young and excited
to see the sun rise
But when I see your sleepy face
and hold your pajamaed body
warm and heavy from a long night's sleep
I find the strength to give today
a chance

MOTHERHOOD HAS TAUGHT ME

THAT LOVE IS NOT

A FEELING

IT IS A BURNING DESIRE

TO TRY A LITTLE HARDER

THAN I DID

YESTERDAY

When I squeeze you
hold your small body in mine
my wounds stop bleeding
and the dull ache of adulthood
for a moment
ceases to throb
you, my child, are the antidote
to this life

What does it mean to be a mother?
Is the role defined by the cleaning,
cooking, scheduling, kissing,
the tired hugs, the stories read?

The truth is that anyone can do that
but not everyone lies awake in the dark
staring at your face
begging the angels
to cover you with their wings.

DEAR MOTHER

As you grow into the person you were meant to be
remember, my love, that it's okay
to slip
fall
fail
cry
lose
come in dead last
sit this one out with your head in your hands

You can't disappoint me as you walk these slippery rocks of life
for I adored you before you knew what medals were
and applauded your heartbeat and first breath as magnificent victories

If there's one truth I want you to know
tuck into your heart and seal with my kiss
it's that I don't love you because you're perfect
I love you because you're mine

On days I don't feel loved
evenings I drown in my solitude
sure that no one's heart will ever flutter
at my presence again
you run into my arms
and remind me
that to someone
I am everything

DEAR MOTHER

To embrace my child

is to feel my entire body come alive

with the kind of love

I thought was only reserved

for fairy tales

How can it be that

the entire world tells me

a million ways that I'm not enough

but you

my child

even if you could

wouldn't change a thing

DEAR MOTHER

To me there is nothing more beautiful

than a tired mother making room on her lap

for a child who wants only to melt

into the safety

of her warmth

I know I may forget this day
how you look in those
little blue overalls
but please God
don't let me ever forget
the sound of my child's
laughter

Motherhood opened up the floodgates
and filled my deepest wells
with watery emotion
leaving me soft
and ready to spill buckets
of salty sentiment
at the slightest provocation
whether it be a baby koala
clinging to his mother's back at the zoo
or a well-worded commercial

For Mother's Day
I don't want you to spend
very much.
Kindly bottle the scent
of our baby's skin
fresh out of the bath
so I can wear it like
perfume.
Wrap his toddlerhood in
shiny paper
topped with a red bow
so that I can return
to any moment I please

after he's flown away
leaving me with only echoes.
I'll also take his giggle
in a golden locket
and six frozen baby kisses
sloppy openmouthed
wet against my cheek
that I can defrost as needed.
And would it be too bold
to ask for a glove
that allows me to always
feel his hand in mine?

When I tell a man

"I love you"

I mean "You make me happy."

When I tell my children

"I love you"

I mean

"I would burn it all down

to warm your feet."

DEAR MOTHER

I weave my love around you, child
a thick warm blanket
stitched with my veins
stuffed with my breath
sealed with my kiss
so that if one day they tell you
you are not good enough
you'll know
they're lying

An angel told me that love

is the most powerful force in the universe

and I didn't believe

until I saw steel bend

wood burn

brick shatter into dust

and a mother at 4:21 a.m., who had already
risen more times than she cared to know,

hear her child's cry

and rise again

You were not born of my body
but from the depths of my heart
my little seedling
planted in the soft earth of my soul
I don't need to own your tangled roots
to water them
No matter what storms may pass
I will be your sun
singing warm melodies as you grow
stalks and leaves reaching toward the clouded sky
green skin against the pale blue and white tomorrow
How blessed I am to have this flower in my garden

children don't just grow up

they also grow out

first spilling out of your arms

then your lap

then their car seats

and clothes

but take heart, love,

because the one thing they

can never grow out of

is your heart

DEAR MOTHER

I want you to grow
sail, fly, soar
but baby
promise me
that every so often
you'll return to the nest
and let me look at your wings

LAUGHTER

THE TODDLER

Once upon an evening early, while I Netflixed weak and surly
Into many a full and mixerless glass of Jack Daniel's poured
While I faded, body rocking, suddenly there came a knocking
And the sound of someone talking, talking when it's time to snore

"'Tis my tod-dl-er, " I muttered, "knocking at my bedroom door,"
And with that, I gently swore

Ah, distinctly I remember, how my hope did so dismember
As the sleepy child entered like a ghost declaring war
Eagerly I wished for the morrow—or a place without such sorrow
Turned my head to heaven wishing, wishing I could sleep some more

Sleep. The rare and radiant maiden whom the toddler made folklore
Never here forevermore
And with that, I gently swore

MOTHERHOOD REQUIRES MORE SACRIFICE THAN I REALIZED
AND EVEN MORE CARBOHYDRATES

If muffin tops
are the best part
mothers are delicious

dear mother,

a moment of silence and respect
for whoever invented leggings
they did it for us

what you lose in sleep

you gain in never

having to buy an alarm clock

again

SHOWERS ARE BOTH

UNDERRATED

AND OVERRATED

AT THE SAME TIME

they say you should do one thing
every day that scares you
today that will be
taking my three-year-old
down the cereal aisle

GIFT IDEAS FOR HER

-sincere apologies

-snuggles without the expectation that it will
 lead to more

-helping without being asked

-doing your own emotional labor

-pajama pants

WHAT A PITY

WHAT A SHAME

WHAT A TRAGEDY

THAT DINNER WON'T MAKE ITSELF

I've never scaled Everest

or jumped out of a plane at 12,000 feet

But I have taken three kids

to the grocery store at five o'clock

so don't tell me I'm not living

dangerously

You don't know frustration
until you've tried to give a toddler
a snack while driving

dear mother,

any scientist worth their degree
will tell you that
groceries need a full day to mature
after purchase

stop for pizza

At some point
I realized
that the most off-putting ingredient
in my recipes
was the amount of effort
I put into making them

IF YOU CAN SAY

"SIT DOWN AND EAT"

FORTY-FIVE TIMES IN FORTY-FIVE MINUTES

YOU'RE READY TO BE A PARENT

BUNMI LADITAN

IS IT EVEN DINNER
IF NOBODY POOPS?

DEAR MOTHER

to make a two-year-old,
combine one puppy
one incontinent octopus
and a single juice box–loving gangster
mix until it starts slapping

BUNMI LADITAN

IF MY LAUNDRY IS NOT ALIVE
HOW DO I FEEL IT JUDGING ME?

42

dear mother,

hoodies are
semi-formal now
you're fine

DEAR MOTHER

I've done the math
and I can hear "mommy"
145 times in a day
before it sounds
like an enema feels

only parents and medical professionals

regularly ask other people

if they have to poop

dear mother,

running up the slide is wrong
unless the park is empty
then it's right

time flies when you're having fun
but when you're putting
a three-year-old to bed
it mostly just laughs

IT'S MY OPINION

THAT CHILDREN SHOULD BE REAR FACING

UNTIL AT LEAST EIGHTEEN

dear mother,

you can never spend too much
on Etsy
anyone who says otherwise
does not love you

DEAR MOTHER

A four-year-old is a cross between
a dictator
and a lamb

Modern parents don't ask babysitters for references

We want to know who you voted for

your rising sign

and your opinion on fruit juice

DEAR MOTHER

dear mother, waking up before the sun again

one day they will be teenagers
and the revenge will be sweet

hold on

TEARS

DEAR MOTHER

On the nights that are too much
what keeps my eyes
and heart open
is knowing that somewhere
out there
another mother is gazing into the moon
doing the exact same thing

There's no such thing as

strong women

or weak women

We're just women

who do what we must

until we can't

It's always the innocent mothers
the ones so earnestly trying
who feel the most guilt
and take their harmless human
shortcomings to bed
tucking them in
for another night of regret

It feels good to cry sometimes
sloppy tears in my empty minivan
overwhelmed
exhausted
wishing someone would say,
"There there, you're just tired,
off to bed with you,"
and rub my back
until my sniffles are calmed
into gentle breaths

DEAR MOTHER

the most exhausting part of

being a mom

is running alongside

your worries

dear mother,

store-bought
is fine

There's no one
mothers love more
than the person who sees us
struggling, sweating, juggling
and silently,
without ceremony,
helps

OH MOTHER

DO NOT WASTE YOUR DAYS

COMPETING

WITH THE PHOTOGRAPHS

OF STRANGERS

Motherhood is a madness I only wish to sink deeper into
for as I admire the scruffy edges of my children
marvel at the unfinished seams of their untempered natures
I realize that I wasn't made for everybody
and that, like my children,
and all rare gems,
I am not common
Motherhood has taught me
that when I depend on fun house filters to feel beautiful
set my steps to the demanding tick tock of their
accomplishment metronome
and let myself marinate in my own cruel comparisons
be rubbed raw by grating expectations
I waste my moment to streak across the black sky
a shooting star
(one minute there, the next gone forever)
soul on pause
suspended by the fear
of being too messy
forgetting
that I've always been
and will always be
the right amount

Your home is enough

with its messy bedrooms

cluttered kitchen

baskets full of mismatched socks

for no adult

has ever looked at their therapist

face forlorn

eyes full of tears

heart broken

and said

"If only the dishes had been done."

YOUR WORTH AS A MOTHER

IS NOT DEFINED

BY THE STATE OF YOUR LIVING ROOM

Nothing's wrong, it's just hard. "This is unbearable," I think as I listen to my children bicker.

It's not yet dawn, but they're awake and their belligerent voices are an assault on my still-sleeping senses.

Nothing's wrong, it's just hard.

My youngest, his cute chubby face hidden by a raggedy stuffed bear, shakes his head furiously at the breakfast in front of him.

I know he's hungry.

I sigh and turn to face the stack of soiled dishes I would have done last night had I not overdrawn on my energy reserves.

Nothing's wrong, it's just hard.

My oldest two tear apart the laundry pile hunting for socks. Despite this being a daily occurrence, I have failed to organize myself and my home.

Maybe today?

Doubtful.

I hurriedly pack lunches healthier than I ate as a child but somehow still not good enough by today's standards. Is string cheese a protein?

Nothing's wrong, it's just hard.

DEAR MOTHER

I put my coat over my pajamas and give my children a once-over, making sure they look like they come from a home with a mother who cares.

Close enough.

If we don't leave now, we'll be late. Someone can't find a shoe. My youngest can't tear himself away from his shows. He's eating now.

Of course he is.

My oldest is lost in worries over a test I wish I'd helped her prepare more for. My middle is lost in the angst of being the middle. Note to self: give her more attention (the positive kind). My keys no longer exist in this dimension.

Nothing's wrong, it's just hard.

Eventually, we all get where we need to go and I'm sipping a warm, sweet drink purchased like a prayer at a drive-thru. The day got going and all it cost me were a few gray hairs.

Nothing's wrong, it's just hard.

Motherhood and life, two dishes messy enough on their own but when combined form a savory, chunky stew: thick and bubbling with potatoes, carrots, herbs and chunks of tender meat in seasoned gravy.

To be eaten at room temperature. With someone in your lap begging for bites, neck outstretched like a baby bird.

Nothing's wrong, it's just hard.

If you can't figure out
a way to share your
parenting choices
without diminishing
those of others
be quiet

DEAR MOTHER

I never realize how tired I am

Until they're in bed

And I collapse

My body no longer having to pretend

to be awake

I want to say sweet things at night
But all that comes out of my mouth
Are my thoughts, unfiltered

I want to end the day gently
But my nerves are all exposed and frayed
Zapping whoever gets too close

I want to be at my best before their souls drift off to wherever they rest
But instead I'm at my worst

DEAR MOTHER

Lie down and wait for me
I call from downstairs
Knowing I'm not coming
Lie down and wait for me
Wait for the day to slough off
My tired body like scales
For my dulled mind to replenish itself as I scroll through my phone
Not thinking, just being, not talking, just being

Just being, what a luxurious existence

Wait for me, I call to the child
And while you're waiting
Fall asleep

I DON'T HATE YOU
I'M JUST TIRED

dear mother,

on the days you can barely pull yourself from bed
head throbbing
eyes sore
from a night of crying
crawl to the kitchen
fix that cup of coffee
and know that you're not
the only broken amazon
making her way through the rainforest

Sometimes we give from the heart

Other times from the bone

Knowing that the quickest way back to one's pillow

is to meet the child where they are

DEAR MOTHER

The hardest task as a mother
is not in the daily picking up
of dirty solo socks or
toys abandoned mid-play
but in the daily picking up of oneself
when the mind, body, and spirit
are weak
and would love nothing more than to
tunnel under the downy bedsheets
into a secret world of silence
pillows, clouds, and coffee

dear mother,

on the days the clouds refuse to part
don't worry about form
take the shortcut
be a bit late
order the pizza
go to drop-off in those flannel pajama pants
be barefaced

while your war may be invisible
it is real
and your only job
is to survive

These days, I prefer to be alone
Not because I dislike people
But because loneliness follows me
Whether anyone is there or not
So at least when I'm alone
Feeling alone
For a moment
I make sense

I live with my back against a bulging door
and on the other side
churning waters rise
but I push back with all of my strength
listening to the frame creak and whine
knowing that any moment it'll all come down
on top of me
drowning me violently
my arms ache
and my knees wobble
as I hold the door

keep holding the door

DEAR MOTHER

dear mother,

on the days the pain is too great
and you dream of flying away
wrap the blanket around yourself
close your eyes
and imagine a future bursting at the seams
with your wildest dreams
let it tickle your psyche
giggle at the preposterousness of it all
and stay

Depression isn't sadness
It's the muting of a spirit
Applause for life held indefinitely
It's the fatigue of young bones
The bitterness of new blood
The sadness is just the wilting garnish
on this empty plate

DEAR MOTHER

In real wars

the enemy speaks a different language

worships a different god

or at least waves a flag of different colors

but in mine

we share the same skin

call the same skull home

and my secrets flow from my heart

to my adversary's ears

how do you fight a battle

when the foe

is tangled within you?

the casualties

are your memories?

how do you know

when you've won?

83

anxiety isn't about being shy
it's your body living in the present
while your mind dwells
amongst your favorite nightmares

DEAR MOTHER

dear mother,

no
they would not
be better off
without
you

In a mother's love

the only heartbreak

is when they do

what you have prepared them for:

leave

DEAR MOTHER

Mothers with invisible children
walk among us

We see the one in her stroller
We see the one in her arms
But the one in her heart is
invisible

Unseen by the world
but as real and loved
as a child can be

dear mother,

you're never alone
I'm right beside you
holding your hand

DEAR MOTHER

You were supposed to be born today
but life had other plans
and so you sit atop
the pillowy white clouds
looking down on a world you never joined

I don't know when you died
when your heart stopped beating inside of me
but I do remember how my heart stopped
upon seeing the blood
and while I never got to hold you in my arms
know that I hold you in my soul
where you float
safe and loved
for eternity

DEAR MOTHER

When night is at its darkest

I try to imagine your face

my heart forlorn

missing someone

I've never met

You're still my child, angel

even though you'll never wear diapers

or ride a bike

You're still my child

even without a first day of school

or a last day of camp

I hear the whisper of your name

on windy fall afternoons

And feel your spirit in the blue butterflies

that rest on my palm

We must live on opposite sides of the veil

for a little while

Wait for me, angel

I won't be long

On those long
laundry-filled
runny-nose
why-are-you-crying-now
days that after fourteen hours
refuse to melt into night
if I listen closely enough
I can hear my great-great-great-grandmothers
chanting my name.

Dear Mother,

While you stand at the stove stirring
bright orange macaroni and cheese from the box
the weight of the world on your chest
the weight of your home on your shoulders
and the weight of each of your children's futures,
rocky paths you can't pave,
on your heart
listen

Inside your soul you will hear angels singing songs
as they drop pale pink flower petals atop your head

These angels exist just for mothers
and all of you have them
Sometimes they gently blow warm rose-scented wind on our necks
three minutes before the baby wakes up
Sometimes they scream into our minds
when the toddler is standing on the back of the couch again
uncoordinated superhero
But most of the time they're just there for you
replenishing
brushing your hair gently
singing lullabies into your empty wells
rocking your tired valleys to sleep

These angels are charged with mothering the mothers
nursing our spirits as we nurse the world entire

MADNESS

the paradox of motherhood
is waiting for bedtime
with the anticipation of a child
longing for Christmas morning
and then
after little eyes have long closed
lying on the couch
smiling at photos of them
on your phone

DEAR MOTHER

When I'm with them
I dream of peace
crave silence
fantasize about beaches
fruity frozen drinks
the only sound being
the sea lapping frothily against the sand
But only a few hours into my
solitude
my heart begins rumbling its hunger
and my body aches
to have their small bodies against mine
feel my lips on their buttery cheeks
What kind of madness is this

BUNMI LADITAN

Nobody tells you

that you will drown in motherhood

smiling and crying

as you sink

into its lovely depths

eternal baptism

DEAR MOTHER

I wish I was your grandmother
rather than your mother
soak you up without the angst
eat you up without the indigestion
love you without the fear
enjoy your childhood
without the second-guessing
and the guilt
already having grown and settled
into the silver-haired woman whose nerves
have long since calmed

There are two mothers inside of me.
One wears flowing skirts
made of pressed flowers and
sewn with spiderweb thread.
Her words are honey soaked
and her arms never tire of holding
babies against her breast.
She breathes in each moment
as if smelling freshly baked
coffee cake
and smiles real smiles.

The second mother wears only
yesterday's pajamas
her skin, hair, and heart are dry
parched
her mind throbs with restless
boredom
as each moment falls on her
like tiny bombs of redundant domesticity.
She stares at her keys
waiting for the moment she can grab them
and run out the door
alone.

It's tempting to hold each moment
up to the sun
examining it for flaws
glaring imperfections
noticing how it fails to meet our expectations
for what it should be, could have been
but what if you put it down
let it wash over you
accept it as yours
make your peace
with the present
acknowledging that it doesn't have to be
perfect
to be
beautiful

DEAR MOTHER

As exhausted as I am
overwhelmed
I know these are the best days
The ones I'll daydream about one day
Wishing there was a way to go back
even if just for an hour

It's tiresome feigning
interest in yet another
hastily scribbled dog or car
until I consider
that one day
without notice
I won't be the first person
he wants to show things to

Some days I feel like the poison
corroding everything I touch
a toxic cloud
Other days I'm the antidote
baking, hugging, being the
mother I want to be
All the while knowing
they deserve so much better

I can get so lost
in the comparison
my thirsty eyes
drinking up the crafted images
we create to celebrate motherhood
and to pretend it's all going
according to plan
that I forget
that it was meant to be messy
it was meant to hurt
because nothing this beautiful
is ever easy

MOTHERHOOD IS THE ONLY TIME
YOU'RE EXPECTED TO LOOK GOOD
WHILE DROWNING

CAMERA ROLL

At the end of the night
when the house is asleep
I scroll through my photos
How do snapshots stir such pining
for moments that have drifted skyward
like cotton-topped dandelion seeds
by life's steady winds?
Moments I fought to exist in
are now stripped of angst
and repainted with the brush of
simple romance and innocence
If only my eyes were cameras

DEAR MOTHER

Sometimes I don't know if I'm going to survive
all of this giving taking asking crying whining

Then they'll look at me
smiling the goofy smile of children
eyes dancing mischievously
cheeks plump off a steady diet of my irritation
ready to burst into the carefree giggles
of a human being who's never paid taxes

In those moments, I can't help but laugh

DEAR MOTHER

He said "Mommy"
too many times
and I nearly snapped
until I realized that
one day
without notice
he'll exchange it for
"Mom"
So until then,
Mommy's here

the magic of motherhood
is how it manages to
drain and fill you
at once
and always when you need it
the most

dear mother,

you don't have to enjoy every moment
life isn't an ice cream cone
it's a buffet
and some of the dishes
are cold

RAISING

SOME DAYS I CAN'T BELIEVE
THEY'RE LETTING ME RAISE HUMANS

MOTHERHOOD HAS A WAY OF TAKING ALL OF YOUR

"I'LL NEVERS" AND TURNING THEM INTO

"WHATEVER WORKS."

dear mother,

trust your gut
your instincts know
what your mind can't explain

The triumph of motherhood cannot be found
in the quest for perfection
It exists solely in the daily decision to—
in the face of fatigue
in the reality that it is not yet dawn
in the knowledge that more mistakes
will be made—
show up

What I'm most afraid of

is failing these children

whose only crime

was choosing me

as their mother

DEAR MOTHER

Every day I have the choice
to make heaven or hell
under this roof
for these angels
And my chest tightens
under the weight of the responsibility
Until I remember
that to them
heaven is French toast

we don't have children

children have us

our hearts bound tightly within their fingers

our dreams painted with their futures

our lives, planets orbiting their hopeful suns

DEAR MOTHER

When the nurse yelled "Push!"
I didn't realize I'd have to do it forever
Push them to take those first steps
Push them to study for that test
Push them to try their best
"How long did you push for?" another mother asks me
I'll let you know when I stop

People seem ordinary
until you consider
that everyone was once a newborn
whose face someone stared into
when they were just seconds old
someone carried them within
felt their soft kicks in the night
someone held a bottle to their lips
and watched them take hungry gulps
so while people are common
they are anything but ordinary
because in this world full of fear
hatred
scarcity
someone loved them enough
to make sure they survived

DEAR MOTHER

dear mother,

you get to decide
because they're your children

Children weren't designed to be

good listeners

because God knows

adults lie

Instead they were made

watchers

expert imitators

so that we can see our truest selves

through the innocent performances

of these small

savage

mimes

I pray they don't notice
my hands shaking
eyes bloated
two sunken ships
from a night of crying
Watch your cartoons
I say in a practiced voice

Too shrill

Mommy's fine
Everything's fine

We can talk to our children about love
explain the intricacies of respect
caution them against relationships
that damage the softest parts of their hearts
but in the end
their greatest teacher
will be what we chose to endure
and why

DEAR MOTHER

The difference between
discipline and abuse
is that with the former
the child may hate you
for a short while
but with the latter
they hate themselves
indefinitely

Whatever soul pains

we as parents do not attempt to heal

we pass on to our children

as an inheritance

bitterness in wicker baskets

but the ones we face

hold up to the sun

sober and afraid

are transformed

by courage and truth

into

legacies

You have my eyes
I pray you don't have my brain
and won't spend a lifetime
battling invisible armies
that march in endless formation
strong relentless soldiers
trained by your secrets
fed a steady diet of your hope

You have my eyes
please let that be all

every once and again
it becomes necessary to
pull out a bucket of soapy water
and a wood-backed bristle
and scrub your childhood
letting the foam run over the memories
wet forgiveness
until it's clean enough
for your children to eat off of

I've learned that the best parents
aren't the ones who
know how to be right
the best ones
are the ones
who know how to
apologize

dear mother,

you're new to this
but
whispers
we all are

if my children grow up to be
nothing but brave and kind
I will consider them a smashing success
because while beauty and wealth are often coveted
and intelligence respected
most of the atrocities in this world
could have been prevented
if more people were simply
brave and kind

Everyone tells you about

The heart-bursting love

Whose explosion

Rains devotions of shrapnel

Forever embedded in your being

For this little baby

But the books don't talk about the guilt

For bringing this beautiful child into a world so broken

A world so evil

A world so painful

What have I done

DEAR MOTHER

I want my children to

take it for granted

as long as they can

for the minute they understand

the value of it all

means the bubble

of safety and love

I have constructed

has popped

I know enough about
the world now
that I question my decision
to bring children into it
But on those days
when the news makes me cry
I look at my baby and hope
that even if it's just for one person
they'll make it a better place

I didn't pray much before having children
But I find myself in the morning asking
whoever gave the swallows their morning song
to watch my babies
May they be invisible to those with bad intentions
and may their faces fall gently
on the eyes and hearts of those
entrusted to care for them

IT'S TAKEN MANY YEARS

BUT I THINK I FINALLY LOVE YOU ENOUGH

TO LET YOU BE YOU

DEAR MOTHER

my wish for you

is that one day

you see yourself

the way I see you

the world doesn't deserve you, child

but it needs you

shine

burn it down

build something better

dear mother,

our daughters watch us
to see what they'll be expected to be
and our sons watch us
to see what they'll be able to get away with

I didn't realize how dangerous it is
to be a woman
until watching my girl grow into one
filled me with equal parts pride
and fear

DEAR MOTHER

Over my dead body
will my son
become a man
who hurts women

I believe these boys

will be better men

because for the first time

we're allowing them to cry

"You can get it yourself,"
I tell my son
and in the distant future
I hear his spouse whisper,
"Thank you."

That moment when your child
Turns a certain way
And you get a glimpse
Of the adult version of their face

DEAR MOTHER

The stillness of a house

pregnant with sleeping children

is like a garden

after a rainstorm has drenched every

last inch

will they remember all the yelling?

or the morning hugs and kisses?

the s'mores on camping trips?

or the massive stack of dishes?

that I was always tired?

or the way a mud pie squishes?

take the best

discard the rest

for that is what my wish is

APOLOGY

Dear children,

I had dreams of the mother I would be
Painted in the hues of honey-glazed roasts and fluffy mashed potatoes

Little did I know that I'd be raising myself along with you
My most difficult child

And so the roasts dissolved into grease-spotted bags of fast food
delivered with a side of steaming guilt
and instead of homemade strawberry tarts dusted with powdered sugar
cooling on a rack in my perfect vintage kitchen
we eat ice cream
from plastic Tupperware
on the couch

Our life is not a magazine spread
Or an Instagram dream
But in lieu of that magic
I give you
Me
Hoping that it's enough

In these days
of autumn apple picking
endless laundry
bedtime stories
chocolate milk afternoons at the park and
morning cuddles, your sleepy body draped on mine like heavy fine linen,
my hope, dear child,
is that your cup may be full
overflowing
with so much golden, sweet, creamy, buttery love
that when you're grown
and people's greedy sips or careless bumps
spill what we've brewed
you'll remember the Play-Doh at the kitchen table
birthday cake for no reason
frosting dotted with rainbow candies
and your heart will grow warm
filling your cup again
and again
forever

DEAR MOTHER

On the bed of my imminent passing
it will not be the gold I've acquired
or applause I've earned
that will bring a peaceful smile to my lips.
My comfort
my courage
will come from knowing
that it was in my heart
that my children found rest.

If I could give you

the promise of a life

without a sea of lonely tears

I would

If I could give you

the promise of a life without

the pain of heartbreak

I would

If I could give you the promise

of a world of justice and peace

I would

But all I can give you are the

soft kiss of my lips

on your forehead

whispers of comfort

in your ears

my arms wrapped

tightly around your

warm body

in the hope that my love

burrows itself into your

bones

So that no matter what may come

you will heal

dear mother,

we can't prevent all of their tears
but we can hold them
while those tears fall

DEAR MOTHER

Some days I wish your heart
still beat within me
so that I could protect you
with my skin
my ribs

But if mother birds can let go
maybe so can I

RISING

Who is going to raise me

while I raise them

Motherhood transforms you into a
Swiss Army knife
A napkin
A task manager
A bag full of solutions
A soft, flesh-covered robot
programmed to anticipate needs
put out fires

Where did I go?

IF I'D KNOWN HOW LONELY

MOTHERHOOD WOULD BE

I WOULD HAVE

BROUGHT A BOOK

What if the children we have are no accident?
Perhaps in the heavens, our souls
embraced in the dewy sparkling expanse
before drawing straws
to decide which one of us would be the parent
and which one the child

I hope I look
as motherly
as other mothers

My motto began as "breast is best"
then melted into "breast is good"
then, after a river's worth of tears
and an afternoon with wise women who survived
despite being burned at the stake of their own expectations,
became "feed the child"

my biggest fear
is that my mind
will always be as messy
as my kitchen counter

motherhood doesn't push you
out of your comfort zone
it takes the comfort zone
blends it with tequila
and forces you to
take shots

dear mother,

your life will get better
when you are able to hand your baby
to someone you trust
and go away for a bit

motherhood exposes
new sources of bliss:
grocery shopping alone
driving alone
bathing alone
peeing alone

because it's only when solitude is rare
that it becomes exponentially sweeter

They say you've made it when the bills all get paid
or report cards are a salad of Bs and As
or when the marriage is just right
or when the house is yea big, just so, sitting in the right zip code

But I tell you now
that no one is happier
than the parent
lost in the unbothered laughter
of their child

DEAR MOTHER

One day you wake up
the same age as your parents
when they had you
and you realize
they never had a chance

I liked you on our first date

was infatuated with you during our first kiss

loved you on our wedding day

But the day my heart was lost forever

to yours

was when I watched you hold

our little one

cradling the product of our devotion

in your arms

DEAR MOTHER

There is nothing that melts the heart
like watching a man whose currency
has always been his strength
exhibit unabashed tenderness
toward a child

the best part of
marriage with kids
is having someone
who's as excited about
the silly things they do
as you are

LOVE IN THE TIME OF CHILDREN

Love under normal circumstances is difficult
But add a baby or two
A toddler or three
And suddenly it feels impossible
Two exhausted, confused hostages
Unable to fight their captors
Reduced to battling each other
With sleep-deprived, clumsy tosses of
Passive-aggressive grenades
Both convinced that if the other would just
Do this
Or do that
Everything would be better, when in fact
All they both want
Is to be reminded
That they,
In this tornado called family,
Still exist
Are still seen
And are still loved

Don't say you love me
if you aren't helping
Because love in the time of children
begins and ends with an empty sink

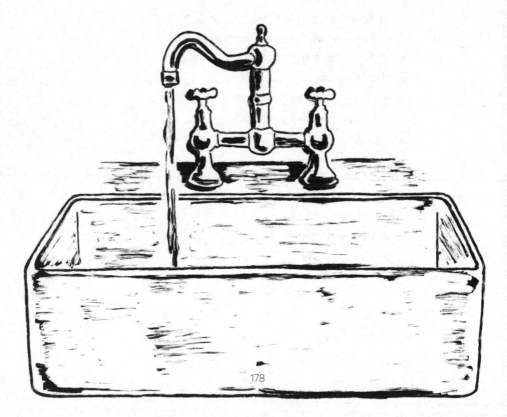

DEAR MOTHER

dear mother,

you are more than a wedding photo
more than a last name
never let a carefully crafted image
become the prison you die in

She is a single mother married
Rich in a male last name
Ring and ceremony
Photos to post
Life orchestrated
But single

Single in the duties it takes
To keep the house going
Working days, scrubbing nights
Single in the child-rearing
Given the occasional afternoon off
As he babysits his children
Reluctantly
She leaves a note
Meal prepared
Diapers out
Won't be long
Making it easy

She is single
in her thoughts
the joys and pains in her heart
unshared in the home
overshared online
Because she's a single mother, married
Her dowry was her dreams
And her reward is an illusion

DEAR MOTHER

dear mother,

tell me about what you're selling
candles, lotion, oils
because I know a woman with her own money
is a woman with options

IF YOU'RE TIRED OF ME
IMAGINE HOW TIRED OF ME
I AM

DEAR MOTHER

if I promise to blame myself
for how I am
will you promise
to stop?

dear mother,

your partner leaving
says more about them
than it does about you

DEAR MOTHER

As much as I want him
need him
I say no
because each time
he turns this home upside down
I am the gate
that cannot afford to be broken

dear mother,

you have permission to leave
the situation that is hurting you
and your babies

Women don't marry for a partner
they marry to have worth
because there's no one society hates or
distrusts more
than a woman without
a man to serve

I don't want to hear about

The flowers he gives you

The vacations you're on

Or the new, beautiful house you're buying

Not because I'm jealous

But because I can imagine those things

Tell me about how you learned to trust

How you make it through life damaged

Because that's where my imagination

Cannot go

My secret desire is for

someone

anyone

to love me as much as I love

these children

dear mother,

you will survive this
new, small apartment
unfamiliar neighborhood
no friends or family
dwindling bank account
cooking from freezer scraps
scrimping on heat
you will survive
just like I did
because you're made of more than flesh and blood
you are made of starlight
and forged in fire

I'M NOT BROKEN

I'M SIMPLY AN ORANGE

IN A BASKET OF APPLES

TRYING MY BEST

TO LOOK RED

From time to time
I find myself
empty-armed
yet swaying
from side to side
or gently bouncing

All that time,
was I comforting my child
or myself?

The unspoken work of motherhood
is keeping one's demons on a leash
pulling them back
muzzling their snarling mouths
slick wet razor sharp teeth
and though our arms might burn
with the constant strain
we hold on

on the day they handed out brains in heaven

I overslept

all that was left was this one

kind enough

but unequipped

not at all calibrated for earth

full of imaginary fears

and major malfunctions

but it was the only one left

so forgive me

I overslept

DEAR MOTHER

Of all the things I pass down to my children
I hope this brain
is not one of them

broken family heirloom

dear mother,

make a necklace out of your guilt
put it in a pretty box
and never wear it again

I wish I could love
Myself as tenderly as I do my children
Forgive myself the way I forgive them
Wrap myself in my own arms
Wipe away my tears
And whisper, "It's okay, I love you"
And believe it

Be careful how you speak about
yourself
for your words will become
your daughter's mother tongue

WHAT A SHAME IT WOULD BE

TO HATE THE BODY

THAT BIRTHED YOUR HEART

When I was younger
with a stomach that held itself in
I felt most beautiful when I looked at my reflection
in the mirror

Now that I'm older
with a tummy that remembers
the souls who passed through it
I feel most beautiful when I look at my reflection
in your eyes

DEAR MOTHER

If babies ruin bodies

we must redefine perfection

because how can ushering life into the world

be done by

anything less than perfect?

Love tore through my body
Leaving it stretched
And dimpled
Unfilled lakes of skin
Long horizontal lines
where you made room for
yourself
Breasts that filled
And emptied
Like the tide
Now rest soft and weary
But proud
Having nourished you
I want to dislike these folds
Frown at the empty
kangaroo pouch
in which my joey's heart
fluttered for the first time
But I can't hate this body
Because it was your home

DEAR MOTHER

I don't like being a mother
any more than a plum tree likes
bearing fruit every summer
deep purple and crimson skinned
spheres of juicy flesh
Motherhood is woven
like colored silk ribbons
into the tapestry of my heart
It is the scent of my
neck and breath
It is the sheen on my skin
And my pulse thrums
to its gentle rhythm
I don't like being a mother
Motherhood is my being

Think of yourself as a garden
Your soul turned over like hard soil
So that seeds of your wildest dreams can be planted
watered by the rain
of your tears
as life picks at the weeds
grabbing at the roots
that which does not belong on your landscape
the thoughts that were strangling you
hindering your growth
stealing your nourishment
Then, after all of this toiling
just when you begin to wonder
if your seeds were rocks
and your patch is destined to be barren forever
an evergreen seedling sprouts
hope

If motherhood has taught me anything
it's that beauty transcends scars
the ones that run like deep oceans
across my abdomen and thighs
it's taught me true strength is soft
a gentle word spoken at 3 a.m.
as my blood boils
and body screams with fatigue
it's taught me joy cannot be bought
but is found in dandelion fields
rain-soaked parks
and unexpected kisses
and for those lessons
precious jewels
I am grateful

BUNMI LADITAN

Labor never ends

because every day

I give birth to

a truer version

of myself

dear mother,

don't care if you breastfeed or not
what your baby's diapers are made out of
if your carpet is visible underneath all of those toys
care about the woman inside of you
the one who existed before
the two lines on the stick
don't let her go